the Christian's Guide to
GUIDANCE

the Christian's Guide to
GUIDANCE

*how to make Biblical decisions
in everyday life*

Jay E. Adams

TIMELESS TEXTS
Woodruff, SC

Unless otherwise noted, Scripture quotations are from The Christian Counselor's New Testament, *by Jay E. Adams, © 1977, 1980 by Jay E. Adams. Revised and Reprinted 1994*

ISBN 1889032-06-9

Contents

Introduction

Just yesterday, a fine Christian couple asked me, "How can we know whether God would have us adopt a child?" Recently, a Christian man puzzled about whether he ought to enter the ministry or look into another sort of work stated that "It is very perplexing! I simply don't know what to do. How can I know?" Still another person wasn't sure whether he ought to propose marriage to a girl he had been dating for over two years. Why? Because he hadn't any assurance that this was the right thing to do.

On the other hand, a Christian said, "With all of these providential circumstances piling up, it is clear that the Lord is directing me to move to another location." And another claims that he had a sense of the Lord's will for him in seeking to begin a church in a certain community. Still another is convinced that even though there has been no confirmation of it in any way, such as a mission board's support, he should go to Ireland as a missionary: "Why, the feeling I got when reading about the need there was so strong it couldn't have been anything other than the Lord's leading."

Both those in the first and those in the second paragraphs are having problems with *guidance*. Those people who were puzzled about what to do would plainly agree with this assessment. Those who were certain they had ascertained the Lord's will in one way or another would hardly think of what they were concluding as a problem. It is my thesis, however, that irrespective of what they may say or think, persons in *both* groups are having a problem with guidance.

The issue is not a minor one. It impinges upon us every day in one way or another. Because guidance has to do with decision-making, it has to do with everything we determine to do. Life is a succession of decisions. The problem crops up in churches regularly as some think they know what ought to be done because (as they say) the Lord has "led" them in the matter, while others have known no such leading and are highly skeptical of those who assert it. On the other hand, those who sense God's will by means of circumstances, promptings in their spirits or strong impressions wonder about the spirituality of those who know nothing of these things. They wonder whether their brothers and sisters who are not subject to "leadings" really believe the Bible as they should, or whether they "limit" God.

Genuinely concerned Christians want to know the facts about this matter because they want to please God by knowing and doing His will. Surely, God has not left us without information concerning this all-important matter. But what has He said? *How can we know* who is correct—those who receive no direct guidance or those who say they do? In this book I intend to answer both of those questions, I hope to your satisfaction—and in such a manner as to open up the whole matter of guidance so that you will be able to make decisions that are pleasing to God.

"A big order," you say? Of course it is. But it is too important to ignore. Too many are confused. Much that is wrong has been said and written about the subject. It is time to set forth clearly and cogently what the Bible teaches. Stay with me over the pages to come as we investigate the issue. The simple fact is that you *can know* God's will.

Chapter One

There is a Problem

Not only do sincere Christians differ about the matter of guidance; even those who claim one sort or another differ as to the *type* of guidance that they report. The matter is truly perplexing. Young Christians, who have only recently come into the faith, may attempt to discern the Lord's will about various matters only to be told one thing by one "older" Christian and something quite different by another. The matter is confusing. Leaders in the same congregation do not always agree on the issue, and many pastors leave the matter up in the air since either they themselves are unclear or they fear upsetting those who disagree with them. The creeds of the church seem silent about the subject and books recounting various experiences abound. Within the same congregation, some people affirm one thing while others affirm another. There are those who warn against any sort of guidance, those who determine every day what shirt, tie, etc. they should select by "promptings," and those who say that you may only know God's general will but not His specific will about detailed matters. A sincere Christian seeking answers is in trouble if he attempts to find unanimity.

Does God direct His people? If so, how does He do it? Those are the two main problems that we shall confront in this book. Mary thought God was directing her to marry Jacob. "The feeling I had toward him could not have come from any other source but God," she said. All her friends, and even a couple of the deacons in her church, thought the marriage was "clearly God's will," though they never said how they reached that conclusion. Yet three years later the marriage was on the rocks, Jacob denied his profession of faith and, in spite of all that her pastor and others did to help, one year later it ended in a messy divorce. So often, people fail to look back and ask the obvious question: was God leading Mary and Jacob into marriage or not? Was Mary right or wrong in thinking so? If, as it seems, Jacob turned out to be an unbeliever, did God guide her into marriage with an unbeliever? If He did, what was His purpose? If He didn't, how did Mary go wrong in discerning God's will? And—to raise only one more question at this point—does God ever guide unbelievers?

Take the case of Jim. Here is a man who thinks that, as a child, he had a call to the mission field. When a pastor asked in his sermon, "How many of you would be willing to forsake all else and go preach the gospel overseas?" Jim raised his hand. Yet, Jim never went. Is it because he was not true to the response that he made when he was eight years old that he is having so many problems now? Is God punishing him? How can he tell? What should he do now that he is settled in a business, has a family of four and has no training for missionary work? Should he pack up his family and head for seminary? Should he consider the raising of his hand the response of an immature child who didn't know what he was doing to a highly emotional sermon in which probably no such appeal should have been made—or what? How can Jim know God's will about this? It troubles him almost every day of his life.

A radio preacher predicted the return of Jesus Christ in the fall of 1994. Carlos and Rosa, who were faithful listeners, believed his reasoning from the Scriptures. Because they thought God was leading them to do so, they sold all that they had and sent it to the preacher to help evangelize others before it was too late. After all, what good would property or money be when Christ would come in less than a year? That was how they saw things. Of course, Christ didn't come and they are left impoverished. The radio preacher no longer had the money; even if they had asked for its return, he would have been likely to say that the decision was strictly their own and he was not responsible for their action. Would he have been right? Was their faith misplaced? Does God accept sincere faith even if it *is* misplaced? Did *God* lead them to give away all that they had? Were they right or wrong in doing so? Everything is in a muddle. How can they know what was right? And, will God bless them in some other way because of their sincerity—in spite of what has happened? What does God want them to do now? This time they want to be absolutely *sure* of God's will before they act. Can they know what it is? If so, how?

Consider one more situation. Bradley has been offered a high paying job. It is plainly a step up from the job that he has at present. However, it will require moving his family to a distant location. His wife Joan is thrilled with the idea. He is not so sure. He has visited the area to which he would have to relocate and can find no good Bible-believing church there. There is one church that is "evangelical," which they probably would have to attend, but the teaching is poor, the doctrine is questionable at points, his children would be raised in a legalistic atmosphere, and he can hardly see anyone challenged by the sort of preaching that he has heard during the recent visit. Joan says, "I am sure the Lord would have you take this job. Think of what it would mean to the children and me. Moreover, we could start a new church and bring a clearer message to the community than they have known heretofore." How can Bradley be sure of God's will in this matter? If he can't, what should he do? Should he consider Joan's certainty about it as "from the Lord," or is she biased by the additional money and the things it would bring to the family? After all, he has no such "leading from God." How is it that she is so sure and he is not? What is he to do under these circumstances? Surely, in some way or other he can know God's will about this matter—can't he?

When I say that there is a problem abroad in the church today about guidance, I am referring to these and many other practical issues that God's people must face from day to day. One person says that guidance comes from a "still small voice," while another maintains that he gets his "leading" from opening the Bible at random and reading what God has to say. In one way or another, God always directs him in that fashion. But what do you do when two persons, say a husband and wife, each claim "leadings"—in opposite directions! At that point you surely can't go by leadings any more; there must be a way of determining whose, if anyone's, "leading" is the true one.

Perhaps you can see, then, that the issue is not only important and impinges on people's everyday lives, but that there is no agreement on the matter— often even among those who claim to understand how God leads them. And, if God leads, does He lead about *everything*? Does He determine which suit I should wear, which car I should buy? Or does He lead in only the larger matters of life? If so, where must one draw the line? What is larger for one person may be smaller for another. How can I know whether to seek guidance about any given matter or not? Should I seek to find God's will in determining which chair to take in the doctor's waiting room or not? Whether I should have dessert with my meal? For that matter, whether I should "eat out" or not? Should I seek His will about such "minute" matters? If not, why not? If not, then at what point do I begin to do so? Is it not important to honor God in all of life? But does honoring Him that way mean asking for guidance about every last decision of life? Wouldn't that impede one in daily living? If not, then about what should I seek guidance? How can I know?

Surely God doesn't intend for us to be confused about guidance. Surely He wants His people to follow His will. Surely God's will can be clearly ascertained. Surely these things are true—but how? *How can I know?* That is the question.

Chapter Two

Does the Bible Teach Guidance?

That God would leave His children without the ability to know what to do, how to ascertain His will and the means for doing so is, on the face of it, unlikely. It is safe to assume that He *must* have arranged for them to receive guidance. How shall we know whether He did in fact do so? Only by examining the matter in the Scriptures where we can find the answers to those questions. That, in a sense, is a circular argument: if we wish to learn about God's revelation we must turn to that biblical revelation in order to do so. Yet, at bottom, all such arguments are circular. That we would go to the Bible for the answer to the question simply means that we (like everyone else) come to such questions with a set of presuppositions, two of which are that there is a God and that if we are to know with certainty anything about Him, ourselves and the world in which we live, we must find such answers in His revelation, the Bible. So the issue is not *whether* the Bible teaches that there is revelation from God; no, the issue simply is of what does that revelation consist, and is it sufficient for the guidance necessary to live a consistent Christian life. In this chapter we intend to begin to investigate that matter.

How can we reason this way? Because we cannot abandon our fundamental Christian commitments (one of which is that the Bible is a revelation from God) and because we can presuppose that those who are reading this book are Christians who share that very same commitment. To abandon faith-commitments would be to dishonor God. We will, therefore, move on to the only questions that remain. What does this biblical revelation tell us about itself with reference to the matters of guidance and the sufficiency thereof? About the answers to these two questions, those who believe that the Bible is a revelation from God differ. Otherwise, we would not have to take the time to discuss these matters.

In this chapter, the first of those two questions is before us: does the Bible teach Guidance? That is to say, does God teach His children in the Bible that He will guide them in the affairs of life? We shall consider at a later point whether the Bible purports to be the only source of guidance from God for us, how the Bible directs us to access the guidance of God, and whether God uses the same means to guide His people at all times.

That God guides His people is, we said, very likely. We can do better than that and we can say, unequivocally, He does. We know that because the Bible—God's infallible, inerrant revelation—says so. In John 16:13 we read, **But when the Spirit of truth comes, He will guide you into all truth.** Truth, of course, is what one needs in order to please God. In the prayer of Jesus for His own, we read, **Sanctify them by the truth; Your word is truth!** (John 17:17) To sanctify means to "set apart" from sin to righteousness, from the old sinful way of life to God's new holy one. Jesus' prayer was effective (cf. my discussion of this verse in *The Christian Counselor's Commentary* on the Gospel of John). In answer to it, we have received the truth Jesus considered necessary to grow spiritually, to be **sanctified**. Whether all the truth we need to guide us in decision making is contained therein, as I said, is not the issue at the moment. That some (or all of what we need) may be found there is without question true because Jesus said the Spirit would **guide** us into **truth** and that it is by this **truth** that **sanctification** is to occur.

In other places, the apostles were told, **I have spoken these things to you so that you won't stumble**[1] (John 16:1). Clearly, Jesus was revealing truth to His apostles so that when they came into times of persecution they would be guided by His prophetic words in such a way that they would make no mistakes about what to do, so that they would be encouraged to do the right things and so that they would know what these things that they were to do and say were. In short, He gave guidance to His disciples even *before* the time they would need it (cf. Matthew 24:25, etc. for additional instances of such prophetic guidance).

---

1. Cf. Matthew 26:31; 13:21 for examples of **stumbling**.

But it was not merely guidance *before* the fact that Jesus promised; He also told the disciples, **When they deliver you up, don't worry about what you will say or how you will say it, because what you will say will be given to you *in that hour*.**[1] That is, guidance about responding in times of persecution would be given precisely when the apostles would need it. Of John the Baptist, his father Zechariah predicted, **You, child, will be called the prophet of the most High . . . to guide our feet into the way of peace** (Luke 1:76,79). Here, it is not the Holy Spirit Who guides directly, but Who will inspire John to guide the people. But however the guidance comes, it seems perfectly clear that God promised guidance to His own.

Do we have any sort of record of how these prophecies were fulfilled? Certainly. We see Peter, Stephen and Paul all relying upon the Holy Spirit Who filled them for the purpose of speaking God's Word. In addition, there are those instances where we are told that the Spirit **spoke** to them and directed them (e.g., Acts 13:2; 16:7; 20:22, 23) There are times when **visions** guided the apostles (Acts 16:9,10); and there is at least one occasion on which, we are told, Jesus **stood by** Paul (Acts 23:11); and there is another on which an angel did the same (Acts 27:23-26). This sort of guidance is certainly direct, explicit and useful for decision-making.

---

1. Matthew 10:19; cf. Mark 13:11; Luke 21:12-15; I John 2:20, 27.

Of course, what we are talking about is God directing those whom He specially set apart for the work of founding His church. This was the direct, inspired guidance given to **prophets and apostles** of whom Paul spoke in Ephesians 2:20, and to which he referred to not merely as guidance but, more specifically, as **revelation** (cf. Ephesians 3:5; since it was guidance from God, it could be nothing but revelatory). These men are separated out from among the four officers of Christ's church mentioned in Ephesians 4:11 presumably because their offices, unlike those of the evangelists and shepherd-teachers, were not to be permanent (there is not even a hint of apostolic succession in the New Testament). When the apostle and other prophets like Luke, Mark, etc. completed their work of revealing God's truth to us by writing the Books of the New Testament, the revelatory **foundation** had been laid. All else would be built on that. It is true that God raised up other prophets in the early church who guided God's congregations before the time when the **complete** will of God had been codified in written form (I Corinthians 14; but see 13:8-10). These prophets only prophesied **in part** (i.e., about particular issues concerning their own congregations) but their partial prophecies were to be **set aside** as incomplete when the **complete** revelation of God would **come**. Plainly, this is the intent of I Corinthians 13:9,10. The context makes that clear: Paul is writing about present, *partial* prophecy and the *future, complete* prophecy that had not yet come. So, the sort of information that directly guided the New Testament congregations into partial truth would be preempted by the complete, full revelation from God that would come *in its place*. That means that there would come a time (as Paul clearly says) when special knowledge, tongues-speaking and prophecy would no longer take place because something better (since complete) would take its place (v. 8). From this information we are able to conclude at least two facts:

1. These means of revelatory guidance were inadequate (**partial**);
2. Such guidance was but temporary, intended to serve individual congregations like Corinth only until a better, **complete**, universal revelation would replace it.[1]

So, what does our examination tell us? It says that God guides His people by means of revelation. That He guided them for a time by direct, partial revelation. That a time would come when the prophets and apostles would have fully laid the foundation upon which Christ's church would be built. And, at

---

1. The words in I Corinthians 13:11,12 are but two illustrations of how incomplete, inadequate, temporary things are superseded by those that are better and complete. There is nothing about the second coming in these verses. Face-to-face is better than looking into a distorted, bronze mirror; adult ways are better than childish ones. These two examples are illustrative of how the complete revelation would replace the partial one. The hymn that speaks about being "face-to-face with Christ my Savior," may have led us astray from the proper interpretation of these verses. It teaches the same truth, of course, that

that time, the partial means of guidance by revelation would be replaced by a permanent one. Presumably, since the apostles and the prophets have passed away, then, we are now living in the time when we have the superior, complete revelation of God to guide us. As we progress, therefore, we must take care to understand exactly what that means.

---

what is face-to-face is better than a mere reflection in a bronze mirror. But there is—I repeat—nothing in the passage to do with the second coming. If it did refer to Christ's return, **hope** would not **remain** (cf. Romans 8:24).

Chapter Three

Some Interesting Facts

We have seen that God promised the apostles the ability to know what to do and what to say in periods of persecution. Moreover, we have seen that He also guided them about where to go, where not to go. The several congregations were granted gifts by the laying on of the apostles' hands (the means by which they received such gifts; cf. Acts 8:17,18; 19:6) through which they could **partially** know God's will, to guide their people during the time before the complete revelation of God would be given. And we also saw that partial prophecy, tongues-speaking and the word of knowledge would all come to an end when the complete revelation was granted.

Now, it is time to understand other facts that grow out of this basic orientation to guidance. First, it is plain that guidance would not cease when the partial revelatory means were replaced. Indeed, the complete revelation that would come was to be a better, fuller, more universal guide to the church of all places and all times. We can be sure, then, that we too receive guidance from God. If the former guidance was partial, but because revelatory, was also inerrant, there is no reason to believe that the complete revelation that we are given is any less so. We are talking, then, about guidance from God, about what we should do as Christians, as *nothing less than inspired.* This is an important point since there are those who think that God's guidance is something less. How could it be if it is truly from God? This is an important fact to keep in mind: God does not give false, poor or even partially true guidance. Whatever God does in guiding His people, by the very fact that He does it, must be true and inerrant. To say that the temporary, partial guidance was inerrant,[1] and that the complete revelatory guidance is not, does not make any sense at all.

While the point that I just made should be obvious, it does not seem to occur to some who claim direct revelation of God's will in one way or another, only to say, in many cases, that they were wrong about it. They escape from saying God was wrong by claiming that they mistakenly thought an experience they had was revelatory guidance. But does God give us direct revelation that we cannot know is such? If so, of what value is it? When the partial revelation given to the early congregations came, everyone knew it was from God because it was spoken by a prophet. When Peter and Paul received revelations from an angel, from a vision or from the Lord Jesus Himself, there was no doubt about it. Are we to think, then, that the discerning of what is God's will today will be less definite? We affirm the opposite: God's will is unequivocally known to be such.

---

1. It was not partially inerrant and partially errant, but partial *only in terms of not being complete.*

It is possible for us to misinterpret, to misuse or to ignore the revelation of God's will. It is possible for us to have learned only part of it, even though it is already complete. But for His children not to know how to determine what is God's revelatory will, or how to access it, is preposterous. When God sets forth His revelatory guidance, He intends us to know and to follow it. He does not hide it from His children. He does not confuse it with something else; He presents it to them complete and clear.

But we have used several terms interchangeably. We have spoken of **guidance**, of **revelation** and of the **revelatory will** of God. It is not difficult to move from the one to the other. They are all terms that speak, in different ways, from various perspectives, of the same thing. The only word that might occasion some difficulty, perhaps, is the word **will**. You will notice that in using the term, I included the qualifier, "revelatory." The reason for this is because the word "will" is used in two senses in the Bible. Sometimes it means that which God from all eternity has decreed to happen. That, we might call God's *decretive* will. But there is another use of the term will: it is also used to mean that which God requires of men. In that sense, we might speak of God's *directive* will. It is of the directive will of God that we speak when we call it His **revelatory will**. The two terms used together make it clear that whatever God *requires*, however He *directs*, in whatever ways that He *guides*, He infallibly tells us to do, think or say something. Of course, we may disobey. And, of course, the **directive** will of God, therefore, unlike His **decretive** will, is not a statement of something that will surely happen. So, while guidance may be given, it may be misunderstood, disobeyed or otherwise not followed.

God's directive will for Adam and Eve was to refrain from eating of the fruit He had marked off limits. They were given clear, inerrant guidance in the matter. But Adam and Eve, though knowing that will, disobeyed and followed the will of another: Satan. They would not be guided by God. Yet, all of those acts (and every other in the history of the world) are a part of His decretive will.[1] It follows, then, that guidance, though infallible, is not necessarily heeded. Though God may guide, we may still fall into problems, stumble in darkness, remain confused. But that is not God's fault; in every instance where a Christian does not know what God wants him to do, it is his own fault. So, having made that clear, we may proceed.

If you have problems believing that God's directive will is available for you, listen to the encouragement He gives you to discover and follow it.

In Colossians 1:9 and 10 Paul prays that we **may be filled with the full knowledge of His will . . . to walk in a way that is worthy of the Lord, pleasing Him in everything, bearing the fruit of every sort**

---

1. For details about the problem of evil as it relates to God's decretive will, see my book *The Grand Demonstration.*

of good work and growing in the full knowledge of God. Would Paul pray for something that is impossible? Of course not! It is possible to know more and more of God's will, and to produce the behavior (**fruit**) He desires more and more consistently in one's life.

In doing so, God **leads** believers into the paths of righteousness for His Name's sake (cf. Psalm 23:3; Galatians 5:16,18). The Holy Spirit leads us by enabling us to **walk** in ways that produce **fruit**. The leading described in Galatians is leading away from the works of the flesh that are listed in verses 19 through 21, and into those called the fruit of the Spirit that are listed in verses 22 and 23. There is no mention in the Bible of leading with reference to such matters as which automobile to buy, etc. The guidance and leading we have encountered has to do with ministry, on the one hand, and righteous living, on the other.

But enough of that. If we today are guided infallibly by God, we must know *how* that guidance takes place. In the next chapter we shall consider some ways that Christians have sought guidance.

Chapter Four

Ways Guidance is Sought

Recently, I visited a Sunday School class of a Bible believing church. The teacher expounded Joshua 9, the story of the Hivites who came from Gibeon. Because they feared the Israelites, they sent delegates requesting Israel to make a treaty with them. These delegates disguised themselves as travelers from a distant land outside the territory Israel had been commanded to occupy. They wore old sandals and threadbare garments, carried old sacks and wineskins, and brought food that was dry and crumbly. They spoke only of victories long past, not recent ones.

The teacher did a good job of reiterating the facts of the incident. Then he went on to apply it to us. Rightly, he showed that God had forbidden His people to make treaties with the people of the land of Palestine (Deut. 7:1-5; 20:16-18). Rightly, he pointed out that the people were deceived by failing to inquire of the Lord (Joshua 9:14[b]), and rightly, he warned us of the deceptions of Satan in leading God's people to violate God's plain commandments.

Then he asked, "How can a Christian know he is making a decision in accord with God's will?" It was, of course, the question of guidance. The question was appropriate, and Joshua 9 has something important to say on this vital subject. His answer was something like this: "I asked my Christian friends and consulted some Christian books, and what I have come up with is that there are six ways in which you can know God's will in reaching a decision." He then wrote his six guidelines on the board as follows:

1. Scripture
2. Prayer
3. Advice of Others
4. Circumstances
5. Reason
6. Peace

Was he correct? No. Five of the ways as he presented them were wrong! Yet, what he taught was by no means unusual. It is the sort of teaching you can find in all sorts of churches today. Because that is true, it will be necessary to consider each guideline in some detail to discover where he went wrong.

Item 1 is the only one that can stand without qualification (and will be discussed later). In his explanation of item 2, the teacher failed to rightly tell us the place of *prayer* in the process of receiving guidance from God. His idea (a very common one, unfortunately) was that when you pray, you must be still and listen for some sort of answer from God. This error echoes J. Oliver Buswell, who wrote, "Our conversation with God is reciprocal. God speaks to us while we pray, though we do not always recognize

His voice."[1] Is God's revelatory guidance so hard to recognize? The New Testament examples of guidance do not give us any indication that this is so. Moreover, where does the Bible speak of prayer as conversational? Conversations, of course, are reciprocal. But prayer in Scripture is always represented as man addressing God; never are we told to listen for an answer in prayer. God speaks in the Bible in answer to our prayers.

If God speaks to us, why were the Israelites to consult the Urim and the Thummim (cf. Num. 27:21)? Moreover, if God whispers answers in stillness, why bother with the other five items? Such replies would be better even than Scripture since they would be in English (we wouldn't have the translation problem from Greek or Hebrew), and they would be directly applied to our individual situations. No, any such idea, even ideas of deep impressions or feelings received in prayerful waiting, must be eliminated.

David Whitney postulates a certain sort of ecstatic experience: "The Holy Spirit guides us in prayer better when we are airborne in prayer than when we are not."[2] Where does anything like that appear in the Bible? What does it mean to be "airborne"? This is the sort of strange teaching that is

---

1. J. O. Buswell, Jr., *Problems in the Prayer Life*, Chicago: Moody Press, 1928, p. 10.
2. Whitney, *Spiritual Discipline*, p. 65.

presented by people who think that prayer is a two way street.

To discover the Lord's will you should pray for help to understand and use the Bible in a proper way. It should be prayer for ability and strength to do whatever you discover God wants of you as you study the Scriptures. We are not given the Urim and Thummim for our day, but we have been given an inerrant and infallible Book, which contains all we need by way of precept and example for living a life pleasing to God. All that is necessary to love God and our neighbor is found, in one form or another, in the Bible. Today we consult God by turning to His written Word.

What of the other four items the teacher listed? Is seeking the advice of others or looking at circumstances helpful when making a decision? Look at what happened to the people of God when they did just that. Joshua listened to advisers who investigated the claims of the Gibeonites, and sinned (Josh. 9:14). Looking at the circumstances—old wineskins, crumbly bread, etc.—was precisely what deceived them. Surely, their reasoning in the situation failed them. And their peace, or assurance that they were doing the right thing, was utterly false. Indeed, if the teacher had stayed with the biblical passage itself rather than consulting his friends, he would have seen that the text is totally opposed to the notion that divine guidance is found by these procedures.

What role should the *advice of others* play in making decisions? God makes no promise to reveal His will through others. While it might be a wise thing to consult with others in order to better analyze the situation in which you find yourself, and in order to get their advice about what the Scriptures say you should do about it, God, not others, must lead you into the paths of righteousness. When others speak from the Bible, however, you should give serious attention to what they say; they may have a better knowledge of God's written revelation than you about certain points. Yet, in the final analysis, you should search the Scriptures (as the Bereans were commended for doing) to see if what your advisors have said about God's Word is true. You must be sure that whatever they advise is truly what God teaches there.

Well, what about the idea of "open or closed doors" (another way to speak of *circumstances*)? True, Paul talks about the Lord opening a door of opportunity for him to preach the gospel. But when he speaks that way, he is talking *after* the fact. And even then, that was no indication that he was to remain there. Indeed, Paul left the great opportunity at Troas and went on to Macedonia. An "open door" is not something that one must always walk through. He prayed also that God would open a door for the Word (Colossians 4:3), but you never hear him (or anyone else) saying, "God showed me His will by opening a door," or "God guides me by opening doors."

It is dangerous to assume God is guiding one into a certain pathway because the circumstances look advantageous. Some open doors lead to elevator shafts! Circumstances are not like sardine cans. If you go camping up in the woods of Canada, but forget your can opener, you are O.K. if you took sardine cans but in serious trouble if you didn't. Why? Sardine cans, characteristically, have a key attached to the bottom. But circumstances are not like that. They do not come with a key to interpret them. Whenever you seek to determine God's will from circumstances, *you* bring the key (the interpretation) to them. That is dangerous; there is no infallible, inerrant, human interpretation of circumstances. Thus God is not guiding by them; remember, His guidance is inerrant.

Suppose you strongly think that you should be a missionary to India. You apply for a visa and are turned down. You are told that India no longer grants visas to missionaries. That is a "closed door." But what does this circumstance tell you? You can interpret it any number of ways. "Well," you could say, "that means God doesn't want me to be a missionary." Or you could say, "OK, God doesn't want me to be a missionary to India; I'll try somewhere else." You might even say, "God is testing me to see if I mean business; I'll go to India if I have to swim!" *Just what guidance does an open or closed door give?* Absolutely none. The position of the "door" must be interpreted, and in the circumstance itself there is nothing to tell you just how to interpret it. So circumstances do not guide; they require careful understanding and are factors in decision-making because the Bible applies to circumstances, but they are not sources of guidance.

Reason must be used in moving from the Scriptures to the problem as you apply biblical teaching to your decision. But the effects of sin on the human mind have been considerable; you must pray that God will enable you to interpret, to apply, and to implement His biblical truth with accuracy. And you must always check your conclusions with the rest of the biblical principles that converge on the issue at hand. Help from the consensus of commentators at this point, when it can be found, ought to be of some value too. Indeed, in the passage studied in the Sunday School class (Joshua 9), looking at the circumstances was what led to the misjudgment. The old wineskins, crumbly bread, etc., deceived the Israelites and *their reasoning* failed them too. Because they reasoned from an incomplete and faulty view of the circumstances, they sinned.

Then there is the question of *peace.* People say, "Well, I have peace about the matter." This is a subjective judgment that may mean you are ignorant of what God's Word teaches so that you do not have a guilty conscience about contemplating (or doing) something or other. It may mean that you have "seared" your conscience with a "hot iron" so that it has ceased to bother you (I Timothy 4:2). But the notion stems from a misinterpretation of Colossians 3:15. When that verse says that the "peace of God" is to rule on a matter, like an umpire having the "final say," the context clearly indicates that Paul is teaching something quite different from what those who seek guidance from peace suggest. Paul is talking not about peace within you, but about peace among the brothers. When you consider a matter in your heart, the final question ought to be, "Will it promote peace in the church?" That is why the rest of verse 15 mentions the fact that each of us is a part of the body. It is why he has been talking in this vein since verse 12. Here is just one more instance of a verse (in this case only a *part* of a verse) being lifted out of context and used for a purpose that it was never intended to serve.

Guidance comes from the Bible, prayerfully used. The advice of others is to be sought, not for their opinions but for their assistance in using the Bible to help you make a decision that honors God. Circumstances affecting a decision must be evaluated with the biblical parameters, and the conclusions of such evaluations must be stated in biblical terms. Reason alone is not to be trusted and must always be subjected to the Bible at every point. Peace has no relevance whatsoever to the matter. The Bible is the source of revelation from God and the only sure guide to pleasing God. Nowhere else can we find His inerrant Word. Why then should we turn to other sources?

So, the advice given in the Sunday School class was flawed. It advocated turning to all sorts of wrong places (except for the advice to go to the Scriptures). Following that advice will land those who do so in more difficulties than they already had.

Chapter Five

More Ideas About Guidance

We have surveyed five common errors about receiving divine guidance. In this chapter we shall investigate more. For instance, there are those who depend on *feelings*. Those who trust in these ways—impressions, promptings and checks in the spirit, etc.—of determining the Lord's will (investigation proves) are all trusting in their feelings.

In a conversation with me, Bill Gothard asked whether I ever received a *prompting* to stop my car while driving along, to get out and to go up to a home and ring the doorbell and witness to the person who answered. I said, "Never." He said, "It happens to me all the time." We discussed this at some length, and he said that the spiritual impressions he received were neither sensory nor cognitive in nature. But if that is so, you couldn't really know when a prompting occurred or what, specifically, you were being prompted to do. If you didn't "know" it cognitively, if you didn't "feel" it by means of your senses then, so far as you are concerned, it didn't happen. I asked him how he could know he had been prompted. His response was, "When you've got it, you know it." Now, that makes no sense to me. At the end of a somewhat lengthy discussion, I could only conclude that he was interpreting feelings as spiritual urgings.

If you are following feelings, how do you know what you feel is from God? There are few things as indefinite and imprecise as a feeling. A feeling is how you perceive your bodily states. But bodily states can be affected by sleep loss, by sickness, by what you ate (or didn't), by the weather, etc. And they change from time to time. How can one determine what is really going on? What makes you think that God is directing you through your feelings? Surely nothing in the Scriptures gives us reason to think that God guides through feelings.

In his book *Spiritual Disciplines,* David Whitney writes, "Sometimes we can't feel the presence of God at all."[1] What I want to know is does one *ever*? God is a Spirit. He does not have a body; He has no physical presence. Because of this, when He wanted to manifest His presence, He caused a fiery pillar or a glorious cloud to appear, so that men could know He was present. You can't "feel" the presence of a Spirit.

One of the newer songs that is popularly sung, *Sweet, Sweet Spirit*, when speaking of persons present, contains a line that reads, "And I know they feel the presence of the Lord." That is impossible. The Lord Jesus is localized in a body that is in heaven. It is bad theology to attribute to that body the power to be everywhere at once. As *Man*, Jesus is not omnipresent. The only way that His presence could be "felt" would be if that physical body were able to

---

1. Whitney, *op. cit.*, p. 65.

be omnipresent. But in another verse, which may be attempting to explain how it is that Christians can "feel" the Lord's presence, we read, "You'll enjoy the Holy Spirit that we feel." If the attempt is to say that we feel the presence of the Lord Jesus as He comes in the Holy Spirit, that is equally as bad. **A spirit**, Jesus Himself said, **doesn't have flesh and bones as you see I have** (Luke 24:39). You cannot feel a spirit—or a spirit's presence. What people feel is the rhythm of the music, the presence of others around them singing, etc., which may give rise to good feelings; you can be sure they do not feel the Lord.

In spite of these facts, Larry Crabb recently wrote, "At one level, I haven't got a clue what I am doing. But I have a couple of central convictions, and I don't think I've ever felt more directly led by the Lord. It leaves me feeling more scared than I ever felt in my life, but also more excited."[1] Crabb wrote these words in explaining his supposed abandonment of his 25 years of counseling practices which, elsewhere, he said were largely "pretense."[2] All I can say about whatever new system he develops is that if he expects to be guided by God in doing so, he is starting off again on the wrong foot. God does not "lead" by *feeling*. Crabb should know better.

---

1. *Christianity Today*, August 14, 1995, p. 17.
2. For details, see my book *Teaching to Observe*, TIMELESS TEXTS, Woodruff, SC, 1995, pp. 16-20.

Jill Briscoe, in her book *There's a Snake in My Garden,* wrote, "I perused the gospel of John. Approaching the end of the book, I still didn't feel I had received any directive. I pleaded, 'Lord, help me to go on reading until I sense Your direction.'"[1] How, I ask you, does one "sense" anything? Through sensations received by his senses, of course. But what sensory messages would she get by reading the Gospel of John? Would they be vibrations? Would she get certain feelings? If so, what would cause them? Feelings are not messages; they are our perceptions of our bodily states. Is that how one is to use the Bible? Is he or she to read along in some Bible book until certain bodily states change in a way that may be *sensed*? I don't read anything about that in the Scriptures. They are to be read for truth.

A later comment by Jill Briscoe explains (?): "I asked the Holy Spirit to tell me when one of the children needed prayer. Perhaps a vulnerable moment at school, a moral danger, a physical need. Over and over again an inner 'bug' would tell me to pray, and then the peace came."[2] What did this inner bug do? Did it tickle as it crawled over her insides? Did it bite? What in the world is she talking about but some feeling that she had convinced herself was the guidance of the Lord to pray. Again, there is no biblical reason to suspect any such thing will happen. When

---

1. p. 80.
2. Op. cit., p. 132.

people convince themselves that this is the way the Lord leads, they will frequently interpret some feeling that they perceive in their bodies (or that they themselves produce) as that leading. It is fine to pray for one's children, and there is probably no wrong time to do so, but it is not right to attribute some inner tickle or bite as God's guidance.

There is a book on guidance entitled *Experiencing God,*[1] by Henry Blackaby and Claude King, that has been widely circulated in recent days. In this book the changes are rung on the word, "sensing." One is guided by sensing God's will, by sensing that He is at work, etc. In addition, many other such ideas are propounded: we must "wait till God shows us what He is about to do" (p. 28). "God speaks by the Holy Spirit through the Bible, prayer, circumstances and the church to reveal Himself" (p. 37). Twenty pages later we read, "God took the initiative to reveal Himself to people by experience" (p. 57). On page 66 they say, "the church sensed . . . felt led." They write, "When God speaks to you in your quiet time immediately write down what He said before you forget" (p. 87). Why not add it to the Bible if it is revelation from God? One of the writers continues, "As I watch the direction the Spirit is leading me to pray, I begin to get a clear indication of what God is saying to me" (p. 89). On page 134 they say that a church in Canada "sensed very clearly." Is there such a thing as a not so

---

1. LifeWay Press, Nashville, 1990.

clear sensing then? Which is God's leading? Both? Then why clearly sometimes and not so clearly at other times? Is God often unclear? On page 137, guidance is described as *feeling* "called." And on page 142 they write, "God gives you specific guidance in sensing a call." It has been a long time since I have read a book containing more misleading ideas about guidance. There is no doubt that this book has the potential to do much harm.

Then there is the view that God gives *signs* which indicate His will for us. This viewpoint is widely propagated even though Jesus taught us that **An evil and adulterous generation seeks a sign** (Matthew 12:39; 16:4). It would seem dangerous, therefore, for anyone to ask the Lord to give a sign as a means of guidance. Yet Jill Briscoe wrote, "We talked and prayed and searched the Scriptures but seemed to be no nearer to a solution. Then we asked God for a sign. 'Let's ask the Lord to show us His will,' Stuart [her husband] said. 'Like Gideon, we'll put out a fleece.' We determined to choose whichever society offered us a house."[1]

"Well, what about Gideon?" you ask. Certainly, we must look into that matter as it appears in Judges 6. God had already given a sign (fire out of rock that burned meat and bread; cf. vv. 17-21). Because of the low state of the people, God was willing to condescend to do so. It was a special case. But,

---

1. Op. cit., p. 44.

even then, Gideon wanted more (indicating Gideon's sorry state as well). He was not satisfied with seeing an angel and having him perform the miracle. And Gideon knew that asking for another sign was wrong. In verse 39 we read how he asks God not to be angry because he wants more signs! Gideon, like many since, wasn't satisfied with God's first miracle in response to his request; he had to ask for a second one. It is like someone flipping a coin who says, "If it comes up heads, I'll do it." But when it does, he tries again, this time saying, "If it comes up tails, I will." How many times is enough?

In a Blondie cartoon, Dagwood Bumstead goes for a walk, and a rake falls in front of him. He says, "Wow! Look at that!" Then he says, "The rake fell in front of me all by itself! It's a sign from heaven!" In box two, his neighbor wonders why he isn't going to play golf. He explains that the sign indicates he should work in the garden instead. But in the following box, as he lays out his garden tools, he finds a golf club mixed with them. Then, in the final box, as he and the neighbor head out in the car to play golf, the neighbor says, "I thought you decided not to play." Dagwood answers, "The second sign from the heavens cancels out the first." How often people today reason the same way!

Then there are *dreams and visions*. Buswell, speaking of visions, said, "This supernatural activity of the Lord did not cease, nor did the promises cease, with the close of the sacred canon."[1] Years ago at a conference in Mittersill, Austria, at which I spoke, Hans Burke, at that time the director of IFES in Switzerland, publicly said that when he did not have time enough to study the Bible for an answer, he asked God for a dream and then interpreted it by Jungian dream analysis. Can you believe such things? Spurgeon commenting on dreams wrote, "What if you did see an apparition or dream, what would it prove? It would prove nothing except that your imagination was morbidly active." Spurgeon's comment was right on the money. God has used dreams in the past, but there is no place in which He has directed you or me to seek revelation through dreams. How would you distinguish those dreams that you experience from night to night (crazy as many of them are) from a supposed revelatory dream sent by God? God has provided no criteria for doing so!

Finally, I want to consider the possibility of *direct revelation*. James Dobson gave an interview to *Virtue* magazine that appeared in the March/April 1981 issue in which he said, "I'd like to share something very personal with your readers, something I feel deeply. The Lord spoke to me at a Christian Bookseller's Association convention in Atlantic City, New Jersey in 1976. He doesn't do that often, but I definitely heard from Him that day. . . . This is what God said to me as I walked through the hall: 'I have

---

1. Op. cit., p. 41.

chosen to make you visible at this time, for My own purposes. In so doing, I have made My people vulnerable to you. I want you to be careful, Jim. Be careful how you behave. Be careful what you say. Don't do anything to damage the kingdom.'"

Now, it is possible that Dobson was so deeply impressed by the fact that he was to be a principal speaker at this conference that he, himself, imagined, thought, or otherwise produced this remarkable experience. But there is no way that the Bible would countenance seeking such an encounter in order to get guidance, and it is not Biblical to think that such direct revelation is possible today. Moreover, Dobson indicates that this is not the only time when he has had the Lord speak to him directly, even though he does say it doesn't happen often. Why did he need such a revelation? Doesn't the Lord tell us all to be careful about how we behave?

J. I. Packer wrote, "If any man's will is to do [God's] will, not only will he know that Jesus and His teaching are from God (John 7:17), but he will be told if he is out of the way."[1] He then quotes Isaiah 30:21 which says, "Your ears shall hear a word behind you, saying, 'This is the way, walk in it.'" Of course that passage speaks of the prophets *who had been silent* (since the people had dismissed them; cf. vv. 9,10) now beginning to prophesy again (v. 20^{b}). Packer is too good a scholar to have neglected the

---

1. J. I. Packer, *Heart to Heart*, p. 199.

context and misconstrued the meaning of this verse. It has nothing whatsoever to do with personal guidance by direct revelation.

In his book *How To Worship Christ,* Joseph Carroll wrote about a woman's prayer life:

> So I asked her, "What time do you rise to seek the Lord?"
>
> She replied, "Oh, that is not my decision. I made a choice long ago that when He wanted to have fellowship with me I was available. There are times when He calls me at five; there are times when He calls me at six. And on occasion, He will call about two o'clock in the morning, I think, just to test me."
>
> Always she would get up, go to her piano stool and worship her Lord.
>
> I asked, "How long do you stay?"
>
> "Oh, that is up to Him. When He tells me to go back to bed, I go back. If He doesn't want me to sleep, I simply stay up." (p. 18)

Well, what sweet fellowship! But where does the Bible indicate that any such detailed, night-by-night directions will be given to God's children? What this woman says is not biblically understandable.

Consider the following and ask yourself, "Is what we are looking at in 'more respectable circles' any different?"

Subjectivism Run Rampant

Finally, on a lighter note, but one which still touches upon the matter of hermeneutics, it would be difficult to find a better example of such than the case of the dispute between one Jim Dunn and the First Congregational Church of Akron, Ohio.

> It seems that Mr. Dunn believed that God told him to go live outside First Congregational. So he took his dog and set up housekeeping in a tent in the front yard of the church. At the time the article appeared from the Associated Press in *The Baton Rouge Morning Advocate*, Mr. Dunn, dog and tent had been in place there for some thirteen months. Mr. Dunn could have used a shelter two blocks from the church, but that was not where God had told him to go. Apparently, he also received some sort of revelation about taking showers—he abstained from such. He refused a new sleeping bag to replace the soiled one he had been using and rejected gifts of food unless the donor specified that it had come in response to God. "I'm not living my will," Mr. Dunn allowed, "I'm living God's will. . . ."
>
> For all that, we prefer Mr. Dunn's clarity of purpose to the muddleheaded idiocy of the Reverend Bob Mollard, the administrative minister for the church, who is reported to have said, "If God called Jim to live in our front yard, who are we to say God didn't."

>Well, Mr. Mollard may have difficulty in say-
>ing that God did not call Jim Dunn to live in
>the front yard of the First Congregational
>Church of Akron, but we have no difficulty at
>all in saying it. Nor do we have any difficulty
>in saying that neither did God call anyone as
>theologically ignorant and incompetent as
>Mr. Mollard to the ministry.[1]

What do you think? The woman who claimed
revelation about when to pray, the radio personality
who claimed God had made him visible at this time
and Mr. Dunn are not all that far removed from one
another. Why believe one and not believe the other?
All three alike could have said, "I'm not living my
will; I'm living God's will." Once you open the route
of special, private revelation, all sorts of chaotic and
confusing claims come traveling along it. A man says
to a woman whom he admires (presumably in all sincerity), "God told me that we should be married."
How is she to respond? Given the thesis, can she do
otherwise and not run the risk of disobeying God—
even though she has no desire or other indication that
she should marry this man? Would she not be more
biblical in replying, "Well, He hasn't told me, and
until He does there will be no marriage!" When the
door to new, special revelation is opened, there is no
telling where the claims to it will end.

---

1. *The Concerned Presbyterian* (Vol. 1, Issue 2), Summer quarter,
1996; p.12.

Finally, take another recent incident. When Charles Stanley's church was trying to decide whether he should stay or leave his pulpit because of a pending divorce, they decided to vote on the issue on a Sunday night. But that morning, according to the *Atlanta Constitution*, October 2, 1995, Stanley said that God told him, "You keep doing what I called you to do, where I called you to do it, until I tell you to do something else." Of course, the congregation voted for him to remain; how could they vote against God?

Direct revelation of the various sorts that I have just described is nowhere in the Bible said to be available to us. Never are we exhorted to seek it. There is no reason to believe that it really comes from God—especially when so often it contradicts what the Bible has said. It is also very convenient if one wants to strongly back up his wishes.

So, what then is the way to find guidance? We shall spend time examining what the Bible says about this in due course. But there are other matters to be dealt with first.

Chapter Six

Well, Then, How *CAN* I Know?

"So far, in this book, you have done little more than raise questions and doubts and debunk errors. I'm beginning to wonder whether there *is* any way to know what God's will is in a given instance. Are you ever going to tell us? If it may be found in none of these ways that you have been refuting, tell me, how *can* I know God's will?"

What you say is true. I have so far spent the lion's share of the time doing just what you said. But, let me assure you, it *is* possible to know God's will. But, first, let me emphasize that what has preceded is important. Unless you are aware of the problems connected with false views of guidance, you may unwittingly fall into them. That so much time and space has had to be devoted to negative matters, I, too, regret; however, the problem is not of my making. The amount of material dealt with is due to the number of errors that are leading the people of God astray. Errors may be many, you see, but truth is always single.

Before we begin to delve into the question before us in a positive way, let me say that, in one sense, I do not blame many Christians who, because they truly desire to please God, have attempted in these ways to discover what God would have them to do. The problem often lies with those who have taught them error, those who have been reluctant to refute it, and those who have been fuzzy about the whole issue. Yet, even so, every believer is responsible to be sure that what he has been taught is true to the Scriptures. Since life *is*, essentially, a series of day-by-day decisions that are either made according to God's will or not, few matters are more important to the sincere Christian than learning how to discern the will of God. You are to be commended if you picked up this book because, frustrated and puzzled about the matter, you are among those who care to know the truth. Without further delay, then, let's begin to consider the matter of biblical guidance.

We have noted Jesus' words recorded in John 17:17 in passing. Now, think about them more concretely. In His prayer for His disciples both then and now, He said, **Sanctify them by the truth; Your word is truth.** In order to know God's will, one must know truth. How is that? Jesus always related truth to life. In this same Gospel He is recorded as teaching, **If you continue in My word, you are really My disciples, and you will know the truth and the truth will free you.** What Jesus was saying is that **truth** from God is what will **free** you from sin and all its consequences (cf. John 8:34, 36). The freedom that comes from saving faith continues (as Paul and Peter made clear) to free one from wrong ideas about living as Christians.[1]

Most of those who have advocated various views of guidance that I have mentioned in the preceding chapters have been right in thinking that the righteous way—the way to avoid sinful living and to promote holy living—is to be found in revelation from God. But John 17:17 makes it clear that Jesus' **word** is the *one* Source of this sanctifying or *freeing* truth of which He speaks. You may turn to no other source. Jesus did not point to various revelatory ways in which one might learn His will; He spoke only of one: **God's Word**. He is the living Word, in Whom the thoughts of God were incarnated (John 1:1ff.). When that Word became flesh, we could see and hear in concrete terms what God was like, what He expects us to become, etc. But there is only one way in which to know about that living Word and His commandments (Matthew 28:20)—through the Bible.

God did not leave us some uncertain tradition by which He expected us to learn His will. He did not tell us to look for signs or to expect whisperings behind our ears. He did not tell us to expect deep impressions, feelings or sensings or to look for promptings and checks in the spirit. Far less did He

---

1. Cf. Romans 6,7; I Peter 1:18 (See my translation and comments on I Peter in the *Christian Counselor's Commentary* for an understanding of this important teaching).

want us to listen for His voice in prayer or at any other time in any manner. No, rather, the things that Jesus did and said (both while here on the earth and after His resurrection and ascension through His apostles) were inscripturated in the Books that we know as the New Testaments. According to Acts 1:1, we are told that in the Gospel of Luke ("the former account") Luke wrote about **all that Jesus *began* to do and teach**. In the original Greek, the position of the word **began** is emphatic, meaning that it is to be stressed in reading (that is why I placed it in italics).

Jesus did not cease acting or teaching after He ascended to the right hand of the Father. Indeed, much of the most valuable teaching that we would need in order to learn God's will was imparted by Him through the writings of the apostles and the prophets, to whom (as we have seen in a previous chapter) was committed the task of recording God's truth under the inspiration of the Holy Spirit. And, in conjunction with the Old Testament Scriptures, their writings are what Jesus called God's **word** (John 17:17). It is, He told us, that word which **sanctifies**. That which is sanctified is set apart to God. The pots and pans in the temple were called holy (another word for "sanctified"). That did not mean they were righteous. Rather, it meant that they were "set apart" for use only in the temple. You could not borrow one from a priest to cook your spaghetti in. So too, those who conform to the Word (the Bible's teaching) will be set apart from others more and more as they continue to do so. God guides, then, *through His Word.*

The word from God is unique. Listen to what Peter wrote about it:

> **Now we didn't follow cleverly invented myths when we made known to you the power and presence of our Lord Jesus Christ; quite to the contrary, we were eyewitnesses of this majesty. He received from God the Father honor and glory when such a voice as this was brought to Him by the majestic glory: "This is My dearly loved Son, toward Whom I am well disposed." Now we heard this voice that was brought from heaven when we were with Him in the holy mountain. So we have all the more assurance in the prophetic word, to which you will do well to pay attention, as to a lamp shining in a dismal place until the day dawns and the morning star rises in your hearts** (II Peter 1:16-19).

Peter is saying that the prophetic word, buttressed by what He, an eyewitness of its fulfillment, writes, is that to which the Christian is to **pay attention**. He does not ask you in one way or another to seek a revelational experience similar to his. It is to the Scriptures that he points you.

In II Timothy 3:15 and 16 Paul also points Timothy (and all who would follow) to the inscripturated word. Because the Scriptures have been **breathed out by God and** [are] **useful for teaching, for con-**

viction, for correction and for disciplined training in righteousness, in order to make the man from God adequate, and to equip him fully for every good task. Note, the Scriptures are said to contain all the truth necessary to produce the changes that are needed in our lives. The four things they do for the believer are: to show him what God requires of him (they **teach** him what he must believe and do; they are his standard); secondly, to convict him of his failures to live up to that standard (showing him his sin); thirdly, to correct him (show him how to get out of the messes he gets himself into); fourthly, to train him in the disciplined ways of righteousness that God requires (so that he will not in the future have to fall into the same sins again). This is the process of sanctification described. And note, just as Jesus said, this is accomplished by the application to life of the truth found in God's word, the Scriptures. Moreover, in three ways in verse 16, Paul clearly says that the Scriptures are *all* that one needs to become sanctified (they are **adequate**, they equip him **fully**, for **every** good task).

In addition to this, we are told that God's **divine power has given us everything for life and godliness through the full knowledge of the One Who called us by His own glory and might (through which He has given to us valuable, indeed, the greatest promises of all . . .)** (II Peter 1:3, 4[a]). If He has already given you **everything necessary for life and godliness** (that is, to find eternal **life** and to live in a way pleasing to Him), *why would you seek more data*? Paul says that *all* we need to change into a life-style that honors God has been provided in the Scriptures, and Peter agrees. As a matter of fact, Peter locates the **full knowledge** that we need to live godly lives in the **promises** God has given. Where may one find these? Only in the Bible. It is **through these** promises, Peter goes on to say, that we become partakers of a new nature that is divinely-given.

A few more passages of Scripture may be mentioned (there are more): I John 2:20 and 27. John reminded his readers that they have **an Anointing from the Holy One and . . . all know the truth** (v. 20). He is talking to the rank-and-file Christian, not to some special class. They **all** have received and, therefore, know the truth. This is the same **truth** of which John wrote in his Gospel. It is the truth which Jesus said would free them. And it was the truth that the Holy Spirit would come to bring. He is called the **Spirit of** *truth* (John 14:17), Who would teach the apostles **everything** and **remind** them of **everything** that He **told** them (John 14:26). He is the one Who would **guide** them into **all truth** (John 16:13). Could words be clearer? Well, perhaps, yes. Listen to I John 2:27, where the rank-and-file Christian is told, **the Anointing that you received from Him remains in you and you don't need anybody to teach you. Rather, since His Anointing teaches you about everything (and is true, and doesn't lie), remain in Him even as He has taught you.** Why did John write these words? He says, **I wrote these things to you about those who are misleading you** (v. 26). He was having the same problem we have today; there were others (in his case, Gnostics) who said they could provide divine truth that was beyond what the Bible teaches. Yet, here, again, it is said that the Anointing (the Holy Spirit) did teach them **about everything**. Nothing more than what the Spirit gave us through the apostolic writings is necessary; what He gave to the early church (and now to us) is **everything** we need for life and godliness.

Is it any wonder, then, that John, dealing with the same problem, warns, **Watch out for yourselves, that you don't lose that which you have worked for, but rather that you may receive a full reward. Everybody who goes beyond, and doesn't remain in the teaching of Christ, doesn't have God. The one who remains in the teaching has both the Father and the Son** (II John 8, 9). It is heretics and apostates from the church of Christ who believe that there is more teaching to be obtained **beyond** that which Jesus gave us through His apostles before and after His cross and ascension. Why, then, would any Christian desire something **beyond** that which he has received through the inspiration of the Holy Spirit, called the Bible? Not only does that not make sense, but according to John, going beyond apostolic truth is dangerous as well. Almost every cult or heresy has asserted that it had revelation in addition to that which God clearly gave in the Bible.

Let me in conclusion say, the Lord Jesus did **not leave you orphans**; He sent His Spirit to give you what you would need through the apostles and through the Anointing Who illumines you. The illumination of the Spirit is His opening of your heart to comprehend that which He has caused the apostles to write. It is not some new, special revelation either to the church as a whole or to individuals privately. What would they need **beyond** the illumination of the word that sanctifies? So, the conclusion of the matter is that if you want to know God's will, if you desire guidance that will enable you to make righteous decisions, then you have a place to turn to—the Bible. It is not that you must seek any other additional course, it is not that you have to somehow get God to talk to you about your problems; no, He has given you all you need, He has **already** guided you in Scripture. Guidance is not a thing of the future, or even of the present; it is a thing of the past.

"But how do I use this already-given guidance found in the Bible? I don't read anything there about the many day-by-day decisions that I am required to make. The Bible doesn't tell me which car to buy, which suit to wear, which sermon to preach. How can I know *these* things?"

Patience! We will get to all of that in due time. But for now, in Chapter Seven, we must first consider one other matter: what I call "The Holding Principle."

Chapter Seven

The Holding Principle

The Holding Principle is found in Romans 14, summarily spelled out in verse 23. There Paul wrote, **But whoever doubts is condemned if he eats, because he doesn't eat in faith, and whatever isn't done in faith is sin.** That, in essence, is the principle. One must act in faith in order not to sin.

There are many situations in which a person isn't altogether sure whether he ought to act in some way or other *because he thinks that doing so might be a sin against God.* If he goes ahead and does it anyway, he surely sins. This is true *even if the action in itself is not wrong.* "How is that?" you ask. Let me explain. Remember Bradley? He was the fellow who had been offered a high paying job. His wife wants him to take it. But it requires a move to a town in which there is no really solid biblical church. Joan, his wife, is sure that she has the Lord's "leading" about the move. Brad, on the other hand, is concerned about the effects of such a move on his spiritual life and that of his family. To leave behind a fine congregation in which the family is growing spiritually, he thinks, might be wrong. It might be a sinful move, motivated by the love of money. Yet, he cannot help asking, "Does God have something better for us there?" He wonders, "Could we be used to form the nucleus for a better church in the town?" All these and a dozen more questions swirl about in his head. He is perplexed. What should he do?

That is where the Holding Principle comes into play. The Lord's decretive will in this matter is clear: he must not make the move unless (or until) he is **fully convinced in his own mind** that it is perfectly right to do so (cf. Romans 14:5[b]). The principle can be stated this way: If it is doubtful, it is dirty.

"But suppose one is doubtful about something that in itself is perfectly right to do. Suppose the only problem is that he doesn't understand God's Word adequately to make that determination? How could he sin if he goes ahead and does it, assuming that there is nothing wrong with the action?" The answer is simple. He will sin if he takes an action that he thinks might be wrong (even if it isn't, *per se*) because his attitude in doing so was sinful. If he thought that the act might be a sin against God, he was willing nevertheless to take it. That is a sinful attitude. He must act in good faith that what he does is right in the Lord's eyes. Otherwise, he sins. Brad must not make the move (at least at this time).

The chapter has to do with the scruples that some young converts to Christianity had. Some thought that vegetarianism was correct (vv. 2-4). Others had problems with the keeping of days (vv. 5,6). Anyone who ate meat who thought it might be a sin, or anyone who failed to keep a day when he thought that by not doing so he might sin, was, indeed, sinning. He was not acting in faith (v. 23). In his uncertainty and doubt, he nevertheless plunged ahead to do something that he believed might displease God. He thereby did displease Him, even though, as we know, the eating of meat is not sinful. The one who failed to observe some day sinned because he thought to do so might displease God. And so, he did thereby displease Him. He sinned. To eat meat offered to idols is not wrong in itself, but if one is tempted toward idolatry thereby (or tempts another) he too sins. So, whatever is not of faith is sin.

The Holding Principle, then, puts the matter on hold. That, of course, is why I call it the Holding Principle. It is a very valuable one to understand if one is to serve Christ properly.

Now, when we say that it puts a matter on hold, that does not mean that, in most cases, one may walk away and forget it. In some, of course, it may be right to do so if one cannot come to a solid conviction that will allow him to take or to reject an action in faith. In Brad's case, he may have been given a date by which to make up his mind. If he is unable to do so, he will lose the opportunity; his company will then settle the matter for him.

But in other actions, the taking of which is not dependent on some date, the matter is different. As Paul makes clear, God expects us to grow, to increase our understanding of His revealed will, and at length to be able to become **fully convinced** in our minds about what is right and what is wrong. That is the goal. The Holding Principle is just that, a principle that puts an action on hold *until one can determine whether it is right or wrong.* It is not a lazy man's way out that precludes the making of personal decisions. God expects each person eventually to come to a decision on the basis of other biblical principles. Notice that the principle is given in the context of weak and young Christians; it is not designed as a substitute for hard study, thought and action. As one's understanding grows, as one comes to a greater knowledge of the Scriptures, he will resolve many of his former doubts in one direction or another. But while he is in the process, he may need to keep many matters on hold.

There is one other point to make. Notice, one is to become fully persuaded **in his own mind**. That is, he must not act because of the persuasion of *others*. Legalistic churches are often composed of people who want someone else to do their thinking for them. They know nothing of the spirit of the Bereans. The authority in the church (usually a domineering pastor) makes all the decisions, lays down extra-biblical rules and demands submission. That is precisely what many want. Once they become a part of such a church they have a hard time ever leaving; they are not taught to think biblically. They do not know how to reach conclusions from biblical principles; they are part of a cookie-cutter subculture. Everyone conforms. All dress and act alike. New ideas are not tolerated, etc. But against all such attitudes, the apostle wrote: **Each person must become fully convinced in his own mind** (v. 5). There is individual responsibility to think through issues and reach individual convictions about doubtful matters. That means study, thought and courage of expression. It does not mean becoming unsubmissive to a church in which authority is rightly asserted; but it does mean that one may not allow others to run his life. He answers to his Lord not only as a part of a church community but also as an individual.

So, with the Holding Principle plainly in mind, let us at last move on to the method God gave us for determining His decretive will.

Chapter Eight

Here's How You Can Know

Let's get right to it! There is only one way that you can know God's decretive will—from the Bible. "But," you say, "I know that there are commandments in the Bible, yet it fails to tell me many things I'd like to know and many that I need to know." Yes and no. The Bible certainly doesn't tell you or me many things that we might like to know; Deuteronomy 29:29 speaks clearly about that. But it also speaks clearly about information you need to know; II Peter 1:3 says that God **has given us everything necessary for life and godliness**. Now, you must believe that or I can go no further with you. Peter does not say that God *will* give us everything necessary to find eternal life and live a godly life in this world; no, exactly *not* that. He says (using the past tense) that God **has** already given that to us. The tense here is the perfect tense. This tense in Greek points to an action in the past that has continuing effects up until the present. It is very clear from this usage that whatever God did to provide us with all things necessary for life and godliness was already done in apostolic times. What did He do?

As we saw in previous chapters, God made it possible for the apostles to remember all that Jesus did and spoke. He also promised His Spirit to guide them into all truth infallibly. These things God did through the ministry of the apostles. It seems clear, therefore, that whatever it is that you and I require to lead godly lives has been given already. We must look back to that; we do not look forward to any sort of future revelation, and personal guidance, etc. We already have been given *all* that is necessary. Those who want *something more* make a serious mistake; they deny what Peter says is true. Instead of looking back to the apostolic witness, they want revelatory experiences of their own today. They look to the present and to the future rather than to the past. What they need is not something more than what God has given them in His all-sufficient revelation, the Bible; what they need is simply more of the something that they already have. They need to learn how to study, apply and implement the biblical teachings that they already possess. This is the heart of the matter.

But what about the claim that the Bible doesn't tell us which automobile to buy, whom to marry, what city to live in, which job to pursue? If it has **all things necessary** to godly living, then why does it have no answers to these sorts of questions? Surely they, and thousands like them, are matters that are very pertinent to living a godly life. The answer to all such concerns is this: the Bible *does* tell you all that you need to know to make decisions about such matters. "It does?" you ask. "Well, where does it do so? I've searched it from stem to stern and I haven't found anything like that." I want to address the problem in some detail in order to explain what I mean.

First, of course, it is true that the Bible doesn't mention every conceivable decision anyone might make. It would be too cumbersome a book to use if it did. Moreover, decisions set in a more modern milieu would have been unintelligible to people of former ages (for instance, what would a Roman do with a section devoted to proper use of computers?). And think about this: suppose that it did attempt to reply to every decision-making situation you must face; how would you know which one applied to you? To do so would mean to envision every possible decision in relation to every possible circumstance in which the one making it might find himself. This would be necessary because circumstances often determine and color the sort of decisions we are called to make. One person's situation when faced with a move like Bradley's will not be exactly like the one that Bradley and Joan face. Perhaps Smith wants to move; his wife does not. That is not the same situation Bradley faces, even though it may have similarities. Moreover, in a third scenario, the parents want to move, have faith that it is the right thing to do, but the children are adverse to the idea. Again, a different circumstance persists. The Bible could never envision and direct itself specifically to each such set of circumstances. That is certainly one reason it does not.

But, you may think, if revelation were continuing, if it were individualized to every person and every situation, there would be no such problem. Is that so? What about Gideon? He wasn't satisfied with what he received; he had to ask for more and then still more. The problem is that we always wonder. Remember the Blondie cartoon! No, if you think about it, the matter of continuing revelation doesn't solve problems at all. What if Bradley's "leading" was the opposite of Joan's? Of course, God wouldn't give contradictory "leadings," but how would one determine whose (if either's) leading was correct? But, we do not have to argue against continuing revelation in our time. That which is **complete** has come, and in it is *everything* **necessary for life and godliness.** Our only problem, then, is to figure out *how* that is so; we must discover what is in the Bible and how to apply it to decision-making situations.

If the Bible does not speak to every situation *directly*, it must do so *indirectly*. That means that there are not only direct, specific commands ("You must not commit adultery") but more general commands, examples and principles that may be applied to all of life in every generation. How much more valuable is a Book like that! It is that approach to guidance that you must understand and use if you wish to learn how to perform **every good task** to which God calls you. Let's think about this matter for a bit.

First, in addition to the Holding Principle, there is the Expediency Principle. Paul writes, **All sorts of things are lawful for me, but everything isn't**

advantageous [expedient] (I Corinthians 6:12). He had the right to do many things, but because of the particular situations that he faced, he found it expedient not to do some of them. It would be more advantageous (useful, prudent, profitable) for the kingdom of God in a given situation, not to do some of those things that it is perfectly all right to do in others. Here, such matters as deference to others, avoiding anything that might offend unnecessarily, questions about whether it is the best choice among many to make, etc., may determine the decision that one makes.

How does the Expediency Principle differ from the Holding Principle? The latter comes into play when one is not sure about the decision to make—whether a particular act may or may not be a sin. The former applies when one knows that he would not sin by taking the action, but for other reasons may refrain from doing so. These "other reasons" govern the decision out of consideration for the outcome: it would be *better* (not necessarily sinful) to do or not do something. Thinking of others, and the effect of his action on them, Paul also wrote, **All sorts of things are lawful, but not all things are advantageous; all sorts of things are lawful, but not all things build up.** (I Corinthians 10:23) Here, the concern is whether what one does builds up others. In the sixth chapter of I Corinthians, he also had said that all sorts of things are lawful but not all advantageous, and then went on to say, **All sorts of things are law-**

ful for me, but I won't be ruled by any of them.
There the principle extends to matters that, becoming
habitual, may take over one's life. For instance, many
have become so enamored with TV that watching
takes over inordinate amounts of time (the same is
true of others who waste time playing computer
games, surfing the Net, etc.). It is **lawful** to use computers, or to watch TV programs, but that is not true
if what is done is not useful to the building up of
one's life (or the life of others) or if it is not profitable
for the kingdom.

Beyond the Expediency Principle lies the whole
range of other principles that are found in the Bible.
It is necessary to learn how to deduce from the commandments, the examples and the principles set forth
there, all sorts of conclusions about matters not specifically addressed. That is what is meant by *indirect*
guidance.

Consider this approach from another angle.
When, for instance, one must decide what clothes to
wear on a given occasion, he turns only to those general principles about modesty and stewardship that
apply to *all* use of clothing. If what he wears falls
within the general biblical rubrics governing such
issues, he may select any combination that he cares
to. The Bible doesn't restrict him from wearing anything other than green striped ties; therefore, he may
wear any color ties he wishes. God did not give him
any further revelation on the subject in the Bible.
Therefore, God expected him to use his own judg-

ment about the matter. If, however, special questions arise ("What should I wear to the formal affair?"), it would be well to consider the matter of expediency as well. It would be better not to stand out as "peculiar" because of one's dress and thereby disgrace the Lord before unbelievers. While under other circumstances, any sort of shirt, with or without ties, might be lawful (i.e., perfectly right in God's sight). But a plaid shirt among others who are all wearing formal attire would be unprofitable to one's witness. The general principles impinge on each specific decision to define the limits of decision-making.

Take one more example. You would like to attend a formal dinner of a certain organization that supports a political party, but the entrance price is $1,000 a plate, and one must wear tux and white tie. When there is not enough money in the till to buy the children new shoes, it would be wrong to do so. It is not wrong to attend formal dinners, to spend money to do so or to buy acceptable togs to wear, *per se*, but because of the principles of stewardship taught in the Scriptures (cf. I Timothy 6), in the case just described it would be wrong to do it.

So, what we are learning from this discussion so far is that *general* principles (**marry . . . but only in the Lord**; I Corinthians 7:39), in addition to highly *specific* ones (**You must not commit adultery**), are the basis for decision-making. That is to say, God guides through Scriptural principles as they apply to any decisions you may have to make. Often a decision will hang on the application of several principles which, together, box in your options. Take an example. A young man has been encouraged by his parents and his grandparents to enter the ministry. He is a Christian. But he is not sure that he should do so. It is every bit as serious an error to be in the ministry when you should not as it is to not go when you should. How can he know what to do? Well, in addition to study of the Bible concerning ministry, he might speak to a minister or two about what is involved, so that he has a pretty good idea of what it is that he is considering. He will look at the need. He will pray about the matter. But, as he studies the qualifications for a minister in I Timothy and Titus, and attempts to meet them, he will have to determine whether or not he could measure up to these since God calls no one to minister who does not. And, he will look within, as he is investigating these matters, to see if there is a growing desire to take up this task (Does he **aspire** to the work? Cf. I Timothy 3:1). When God gives gifts to His children, He expects them to be developed and deployed. So, he will look at these, work at sharpening them and attempt to put them to use. If he thinks that God is blessing their use, he will take that fact into consideration. He will at length, initially and after graduation from seminary, submit the matter to the church to see if others (officially designated to do so) would encourage him in these pursuits. Finally, he will stand the test of ordination. This decision, then, involves time, effort, study, prayer and consideration at every stage along the way. Many important factors designed to help him decide converge.

Now, two ancillary factors must be mentioned. If that is how God guides, you must become acquainted with the Bible, must be able to use concordances, etc. It implies serious Bible study on your part. The second is this: God expects you to think. He has given you His Spirit to enable you to understand the Scriptures. Why? So that you might use them in such ways. God will not directly tell you what to do, making your decisions for you, because He has already told you how to discover what to do. He has given sufficient general directions for you to make good decisions, and He expects *you* to do so *yourself*. He will not redo for you what He has done already for *all*. There is a hint of self-importance in some who will settle for nothing but individual, private guidance from God!

"But," you protest, "to obtain answers by using general principles to determine specific matters in the way you have described is difficult. Suppose I slip a cog or two when trying to reach a decision? And I wonder: if that is the way things must be determined, can I ever really know beforehand what God wants me to do?" Two good questions.

You may know God's will for you about a specific matter if, in doing so, the general principles apply quite particularly to the situation. Some, of course, do. For instance, I quoted I Corinthians 7 where Paul says that one must marry only in the Lord. That is to say, he may not marry an unbeliever. If a believer was considering doing so, he should be brought to a screeching halt by studying that verse. He would be able to apply it directly to Mary, who has never made a profession of faith in Jesus Christ. But, if later on, Jane and Sally come into his life, it is a different matter altogether. Both of these girls are lovely Christians, both are spiritually growing and mature and both he believes would say "yes" if he asked them to marry him (there is where he might be wrong!); he is at liberty to ask either. The commandment in I Corinthians 7 doesn't further limit his choice. It does not say, "You may marry only girls named 'Jane.'" All other things being equal (often other things are not) he could not be wrong in asking either girl. Yet, there are other matters which may not be so clear. One may be considering entering the ministry, as I indicated above. That decision takes time, testing and approval from the Church of Christ in order to determine whether he should or should not do so. There have been many who have attempted this who *have* made wrong decisions—or at least three or four congregations eventually said so! Because we still are sinners, we and others (presbyteries that test and ordain men for the ministry, for instance) make errors. There must be a willingness to *continue* to examine and reexamine such decisions after they are made, in order to see if there was some error along the way. Some decisions, then, are made *only according to one's best ability to do so*, realizing that what is done is tentative and always open to further consideration. You may not like that, but it is exactly the way that God often leads—one step at a time.

It is altogether possible that God may lead one into preparation for the ministry, for instance, so that he will obtain the training that a seminary affords in order to provide training that later on will enable him to teach at a Christian college, to become a vital, knowledgeable elder in a congregation or for some other ancillary purpose. If God is leading—even in a circuitous way (as he led Moses, Joseph and Daniel to their places of service)—we should not think that there was a mistake on *His* part even if the individual made a mistake in interpreting where God was leading him as he prepared for something else than that which God had intended for him. That is one of the exciting facts about God's guidance. *He* knows where He is taking you, even if (as in the case of Abraham as he left Ur) *you* don't. Much of God's guidance, then, is an adventure in walking with Him. Those who like everything neat, pat and nailed down tightly may have a time with this. But it is something that we all must learn not only to accept and live by, but to become excited about.

So, let's be clear about it. Some guidance is explicit: **Don't worry about anything, but instead in everything, by prayer and by petition with thanksgiving make your requests known to God**

(Philippians 4:6). The words **anything** and **everything** are *absolutes*. They cover all cases. They allow for no exceptions. You do not have to determine when you may and when you may not worry. You *never* may worry. There can be no doubt about God's will in the matter.

Some guidance is not so explicit: Bradley may determine not to make the move to the town in which there is no good church, for the sake of the family and on the basis of the Holding Principle. But, as the family considers the matter over the next year, since no one has filled the position yet, and the company is holding forth even greater inducements for them to go, they decide to investigate the matter further. They talk to their pastor about the question. He decides to call up their denominational center for Home Missions to see if there is any interest in starting a congregation there. The upshot of this is that not only is there interest, but over the year several others have moved to the vicinity who have similar interests. Since the time when they previously considered the move, and turned it down, the situation has changed radically. In fact, since he called, the Committee on Home Missions has challenged their pastor to consider becoming the mission developer in the area. He is willing to accept. Bradley now sees no reason for not moving, and the company is pleased. What has happened? God has honored their previous decision because it was genuine and Bible-based. God's guidance is often progressive in nature. The decision one year ago was made not to move. In a sense it was a test. Bradley's family passed the test. They did not move because they thought to do so might be sin. But, having passed the test, in the providence of God, much more was in store for the family that (at that time) turned down a lucrative advance in salary in order to obey the Lord. Now, the Lord has provided not only a greater salary, but other people and a pastor to begin a new testimony to His grace. And in gratitude, Bradley's family has determined to dedicate the additional funds that they will now earn, in addition to their tithe, to helping that new work begin. You can see how God works, can't you? Matters are not always so clear-cut at first. Sometimes, as in the case of Joseph, they are not so clear-cut for a long time! Joseph could not have uttered the words of Genesis 50:20 until late in his life. Paul could not have written Philippians 1:12 and following until it became clear why God had placed him in prison in Rome. In other cases, such clear-cut indications of what God has in mind may not appear until eternity. That is God's business. It is ours to be genuine, to be faithful and to use all the principles of the Scriptures to please Him by doing His will so far as we are able to discern it at the moment (cf. I Corinthians 4:2).

"Wow! I never thought of following God's will that way! I thought everything should be cut-and-dried. You are actually talking about something very different from that which I ever considered." Well, in one sense I can understand how it may seem frightening (especially to those who always like to have their ducks in a row), but you shouldn't view it that way. Loosen up! Look on living with God as an adventure. Seek to please Him at every turn, doing His will so far as you understand how His Word applies to your circumstances (correcting your course as need be on more fully learning truth from His Word). Even your failures, your mistakes, your misinterpretations, your lack of understanding can be used to lead you to the place where God wants you. After all, He teaches, **Where sin abounded, grace far more abounded** (Romans 5:20[b]). Because His **grace** brings you to repentance, because by His **grace** He may motivate you to study more faithfully, etc., He can even use the wrong things you do to bring about right ends.

Now to say such things is not to open a door for sin, for laziness or for sloppiness. The Lord commended the Berean Jews for their concern to know what He says in the Scriptures (Acts 17:10-12; incidentally, they did not ask for a sign, an impression, a prompting or any such thing. They searched the Scriptures to see if what Paul and Silas said was true.). One may not lead an indolent life and expect God to make up for it. No, that is not the meaning of Romans 5:20. What it does teach, however, is that God's grace is (as the hymn puts it) *greater* than all our sin. The years that the locust has eaten may not only be restored, but may be even more than restored by God's grace. Nothing that happens in a Christian's life is unredeemable. God's grace is so great! So, to bring this all-important chapter to a conclusion, we may say, God leads directly, but He also leads indirectly. Some decisions are made instantaneously, others may be put on hold. Some are made in stages, as one moves from one to another. But in it all, the leading of God is like the leading of the sheep in Psalm 23. Sometimes He takes you through the valley where, in the shadows, death from a wild beast lurks. That drives you closer to Him for protection. Sometimes He leads you beside the quiet waters and tells you to lie down on the green grass. That moves you closer to Him in gratitude. But wherever it may be, whatever you may be doing, He is with you, bringing you back from your wanderings, teaching you His will, bringing you closer to Himself. God's guidance is intended to be a joy, not a burden! Can you begin to see it as such? If so, you will find peace, joy and happiness in the study and application of the Scriptures.[1] They will become for you what they were intended to be: **a light for your feet and a lamp for your way** (Psalm 119:105).

---

1. It is impossible for me to provide a method for the study, application and implementation of the Scriptures in this book. It is also unnecessary. I have written a book, published by Timeless Texts, entitled *What to do on Thursday*, that does just that. The problem is that most of our Scriptural study is intended to help us pass next Sunday's Bible quiz. It fails to direct how to move from the problems that we encounter on Thursday (or any other day of the week) to the Scriptures to find answers to them. And it fails to show us how to apply and implement them. My book is intended to do so. It forms a companion volume to this book on guidance.

Chapter Nine

Objections

All right! I know that there are many objections that must come to mind. But I want to raise and reply to two. The problems you may have can probably be summed up as follows: "I thought guidance was *immediate* and *definitive*."

Doesn't God give instant answers? Well, I've been trying to explain that sometimes He does and sometimes He doesn't. And the difference between those times when He does and when He doesn't depends on His sovereign purposes. Even though the Jews in Berea were **more noble than those in Thessalonica**, they received no instantaneous "leading" from God. Indeed, they had to **search the Scriptures daily** in order to decide whether to believe and follow Paul and Silas' teaching or not. And, it was that very searching that is commended. Why didn't they receive a "warm feeling" as they heard them preach? Or why were they not able to "sense" the truth of what they said? How come they didn't "put out the fleece" to discover God's will about it? Why wasn't there a vision or a dream given to them? Well, you see, Jesus says that **an evil and adulterous generation seeks a sign**, and God commends those who **search the Scriptures daily** for guidance. It is time that people recognize that the signs Jesus gave when on earth were sufficient. That is why John says, **These are written so that you may believe that Jesus is the Christ, God's Son, and that by believing you may have eternal life in His name** (John 20:31). John, who had seen the signs, and reported them in his gospel, nevertheless, asked no one to seek more, other or different signs in order to determine whether Jesus is the Savior. Instead, he pointed them to the Bible—the very gospel that he had written. He is in complete accord with the words of Acts 17:10-12. "But, that had to do with coming to Christ; it didn't pertain to the guidance that Christians receive." Well, I don't think that the Bible makes any such distinction, but if you wish to, let me ask you, which is the most important "leading, guidance" (or whatever you want to call it)? Is it the leading that Jesus spoke of when He said the Father would draw all sorts of people to Him or some other? Surely, salvation is the most important boon anyone may ever receive.

But, let's look at what John says about the guidance of believers. In I John 5:13, he says, **I have written these things to you who believe in the Name of God's Son that you may know that you have eternal life.** How can one know? By feelings? By some direct revelation of the fact? By a still small voice? How? None of the above; he may know by turning to I John and discovering what God says about the matter there.

Jesus had other strong words about the desire to

see confirmatory signs. In Luke 16, you read His story of Lazarus and the rich man. When the latter begged that Abraham send Lazarus from the dead to warn his five brothers about his suffering in hell, Abraham rejected the idea. Instead of this sign, or any other direct revelatory means of learning God's will for them, he emphatically said, **They have Moses and the Prophets [the Old Testament Scriptures]; let them listen to them** (v. 29). But the rich man insists (as do some today who are not satisfied with the Scriptures), **No, Father Abraham. But if somebody from the dead goes to them, they will repent** (v. 30). Then, decisively, Abraham replies, **If they won't listen to Moses and the Prophets, they won't be persuaded even if somebody rises from the dead** (v. 31). The reply is brilliant. Even when Jesus rose from the dead, such persons refused to believe. And there is still an element of that disbelief in every Christian (none of us is perfect in this life). Gideon was not satisfied with one sign; he had to have two more! How often people (not all) who claim such direct guidance have a hard time believing their hunches, feelings, sensings, promptings enough to straightforwardly follow them! Unfortunately, some do, often to their chagrin ultimately. And when Jesus said people err in their ideas of God and His ways with men, it was not to the misinterpretation of some personal revelation that He pointed, but rather, He said, **You are mistaken because you don't know either the Scriptures or God's power** (Matthew

22:29). If they had known the Scriptures, they would have known about God's power.

There is no question that the Scriptures were given to provide **truth** that leads to **sanctification** (John 17:17) and that the changes we must make in our lives are brought about by the power of the Holy Spirit working through them to **teach**, to **convict**, to **correct**, and to **discipline** in God's ways of righteousness (II Timothy 3:16). And Paul makes it absolutely clear, by saying it three ways, that the Bible is sufficient to do this (cf. v. 17). And, remember the words of II Peter 1:3 and 4 in which we are told that God's biblical promises contain "everything necessary for life and godliness."

Since these things are true, I am afraid that you, like the noble Berean Jews, must take the time and make the effort to search the Scriptures daily to discover God's will, and to receive God's guidance. Because that may take some time and some effort, you may not always receive the guidance you desire instantaneously. Those who have failed to spend time in serious study of the Bible in the past will find this disconcerting. May that very fact drive them to spend the time and make the effort in the future!

But what of the second matter—what I have been teaching (especially in Chapter Eight) is that often you will not receive definitive guidance. Many Christians not only want guidance, and want it now; they also want guidance so definitive that there can be no doubt about it. I have said that sometimes it takes a while to learn what God wants because we are not well-enough acquainted with God's word. I have also said that the young Christian must often put decisions on hold because he is not yet **fully persuaded in his own mind** as to what God's word is teaching (cf. our discussion of that important matter in Chapter Seven; and what is true of the young Christian may also hold true of more mature Christians whenever they come up against new decisions they have never had to face before). But there are those who not only want instant guidance, they want it utterly clear-cut and decisive.

Well, that is not the way that guidance often comes (though it does sometimes). Even Paul, who (as an apostle) was the recipient of special, direct revelation, didn't receive it all the time. When he didn't, he too was from time to time "puzzled" about what to do next (cf. II Corinthians 4:8 where the word *aporoumenoi* is used. This word means "perplexed, in doubt, puzzled," even "at one's wit's end."). Why would any Christian today not expect to face issues about which he is not sure what God would have him to do, if Paul had such problems? As a matter of fact, in this same letter he tells us that he totally misinterpreted a situation. He says that on one occasion, things were getting so bad as he ministered in Asia that he **passed the sentence of death** on himself (II Corinthians 1:9). That is a graphic way of saying that he was sure that he would die. He expected no deliverance whatsoever; yet, at length, it came (v. 10). He thought God was preparing him for death, whereas, afterward, revising that view, he understood that the trial was given **so that we wouldn't depend on ourselves but on God** (v. 9). Here is Paul, the apostle who was sold out to the will of God if ever anyone was, changing his mind about what God was doing in his life. Much of what Paul is explaining to the Corinthians is that he changed his plans (cf. 1:12ff.), not because he was fickle (as the false teachers had accused him of being) but for good reasons. He planned carefully (vv. 16,17), but because of what he learned about the church, he altered those plans out of concern for them (vv. 23,24). In this, where is that decisive leading that so many desire or claim? Is there one will of God that Paul received as guidance ("Go to Corinth") by which he made plans that he should carry out at all costs? No, Paul made his own plans (there is nothing said about definitive, decisive guidance) on the basis of the biblical principles that he understood and applied to his work, but was willing to change them when new facts came into play. I am afraid that you will have to do the same if you intend to be biblical. Perhaps it would be easier on you to have it all delivered to you on a silver platter, but God isn't in the business of making things easier. He is working in you to conform you to the image of Jesus Christ. That will take pruning by the Word. It will take prayerful study, time and effort. It will involve your mind.

There is no formula by which you can be assured of guidance. Some have attempted to set forth recipes for obtaining guidance. Here is one very famous one followed by many Christians:

"First, seek to get your heart in such a condition that it has no will of its own in regard to a given matter. Do not depend upon feelings or impressions." [So far, we may say that the second element in the formula is sound advice. But can any believer reach the state of pure perfection that the first element in the formula presupposes? Surely not. Already, then, we have problems. Moreover, what is wrong with expressing your desires to God as David and all the Psalmists did—and even Jesus did, when He asked if the cup might be removed?]

Next, we are advised, "seek the will of the Spirit of God through, or in connection with, the Word of God." [That is a strange statement. What does it mean to find God's will "through or in connection with" the Bible? Why not be clear about this and say by studying the Bible and applying it to the matter at hand? Something other than or less than that seems to be in view. It sounds mystical, and at best is confusing.]

"Take into account providential circumstances." [I have already shown how circumstances do not come with a key, like sardine cans, by which you may open up their "meaning."]

"Ask God in prayer to reveal His will clearly." [But He has already revealed it in the Bible.]

The one who composed this formula went on to say, "Thus through prayer to God, the study of His

Word, and reflection, I come to a deliberate judgment, and if my mind is thus at peace [I also dealt
with that earlier] and continues so after two or three
more petitions [why, there we have Gideon and Dagwood Bumstead all over again, unsure until the coin
has been flipped multiple times], I proceed accord-
ingly. I have found this method always effective."[1]

Give some thought to this matter. Study the Bible
to see if what I have written is so. But don't settle for
formulas, even though they come from people you
may respect. Surely God blesses His children even in
spite of their sins and errors. He is gracious and long-
suffering. And He is working His purposes in this
world, often in spite of our foolishness.

---

1. But where does one find "this method" of George Mueller's in the
Bible?

Chapter Ten

Conclusion

We have set forth what may not be a popular view of guidance. It challenges all of the get-guidance-quick schemes. It sets forth the need to exert prayerful effort in the study and application of the Scriptures as the only way to be sure that one is being truly guided by God. It does not lay out some recipe or formula that is easy to follow. It also promises no immediate guidance in many cases, but only progressive stages in which guidance takes place. Yet, this is the biblical and the historical, reformation view. The Westminster Confession of Faith, for instance, says this:

> The whole counsel of God, concerning all things necessary for his own glory, man's salvation, faith and life, is either expressly set down in Scripture, or by good and necessary consequence may be deduced from Scripture: unto which nothing at any time is to be added, whether by new revelations of the Spirit or traditions of men[1].

As you can see, this is precisely the approach to guidance that we have taken. It is the historic view which has, only in more modern times, been chal-

---

1. *WCF,* 1:6.

lenged by the others that we have rejected as unbiblical. The reformers who reached these conclusions were devout men, wholly committed to the Scriptures for their faith and practice, and finished scholars. While no one should place his faith in men, on the other hand it is nothing short of arrogance that casts aside the work of many such persons lightly in favor of some new ideas, without seriously considering their viewpoint. This is especially true since there is no *one* alternative viewpoint, but many quite different and often conflicting ones. The alternative is not very attractive when considered from this perspective.

Though there are differences, as I indicated in the last paragraph, there is also one similarity. The problem with all of these anti-reformation schemes is that those who propound them, and those who all too readily adopt them, expect God to make their decisions for them. (Remember the woman who said, "That's not my decision"? She expressed it clearly.) There is no way of determining which of these many alternatives is correct; but it should be plain from our study that it is possible to show where they have all gone wrong. God expects you to make decisions. He nowhere teaches quietism. It is always responsible human action energized by the Spirit using His Word that the Bible sets forth as God's way of working. Never self-help or, on the opposite extreme, self-helplessness.

The conclusion of the matter is that unless God

has spoken specifically in the Bible, you *cannot* know His will beyond the general principles that are taught in the Bible. Even Paul, a man who received revelation at times, wrote to Philemon (vs.15), **Perhaps, then, this is why he left you for an hour— that you might have him back forever.** People who adopt modern schemes will not settle for a "perhaps." But Paul, an apostle, would not presume to assert that what he said assuredly was so. He too, when not receiving apostolic revelation, was no more certain about God's decretive will than any of the rest of us. Those who mean well, but have gone astray, have done so for that very reason: they confuse and confound the decretive will of God with his directive one. They can know the latter, but not the former (before the event occurs).

This book has not been written to stir up controversy. As a biblical counselor, I have over and over again seen the havoc non-reformational views of guidance have caused. And I have seen, when people depart from the Bible as the source of guidance, how far astray from it they soon may wander. My purpose, then, has been to check the trend toward these new views and to help people return to the Biblical one.

A final word: The Bible is called **God's law** (*torah*). The word *torah* comes from a figure that means "to thrust out the finger" in order to point the way. That says it all: Scripture is God's way of guidance. There is no other.

Other Titles by Dr. Jay Adams

available from your bookstore or
directly from TIMELESS TEXTS
1-800-814-1045

The Christian Counselor's Commentary Series
by Jay E. Adams   all volumes hardback

Vol. 1—I & II Corinthians
Vol. 2—Galatians, Ephesians, Colossians & Philemon
Vol. 3—I & II Timothy and Titus
Vol. 4—Romans, Philippians, and I & II Thessalonians
Vol. 5—Hebrews, James, I & II Peter, and Jude
Vol. 6—Proverbs

> This series of commentaries is written in everyday English. A must for the layman as well as the Pastor/Counselor. Dr. Adams' everyman style of communication brings forth these biblical truths in a clear understandable way that typifies his writings. He does not try to duplicate the standard, more technical types of commentaries but supplements them with the implications of the text for God-honoring counseling and Christian living.

The Christian Counselor's New Testament
translated by Jay E. Adams   leather & synthetic bindings

> A special translation by Dr. Adams with extensive footnotes and topical side columns. This Bible was specially designed to help the Christian in study as well as counseling. *The Christian Counselor's New Testament* is very user friendly. It leads you through those tough counseling topics by using the Margin Notations and Notation Index for the topic or related topics. Easily used during the counseling session.

A Call for Discernment—
Distinguishing Truth from Error in Today's Church
by Jay E. Adams   142pp. paperback

> Dr. Adams shows the seriousness of the problem of lack of discernment and the effect on Christian lives. *A Call For Discernment* will help you become a more discerning Christian today.

Back to the Blackboard—
Design for a Biblical Christian School
by Jay E. Adams   160pp. paperback

> With curriculum in the courtroom and parents up in arms, education is in the forefront of discussion in much of America today. Here is a truly provocative book on what qualifies as Christian education. These ideas are also very adaptable for the home schooler.

What to do on Thursday—
A Layman's Guide to the Practical Use of the Scriptures
by Jay E. Adams   144pp. paperback

> The Bible has the answers, but can you find, understand and apply them? *What to do on Thursday* teaches you how to study and interpret your Bible to answer the questions that arise all week at work, at play, at home, and at school.

> Dr. Adams has written this study to prepare you to meet the challenges of this fast-moving world with decisions that will honor God. The practical use of the Scriptures on an everyday basis is crucial to all of God's people. You can't wait for your pastor to preach a sermon that applies to your need now. *What to do on Thursday* will help you prepare a template of priorities that will order your life in a Godly pattern.

Teaching to Observe—The Counselor as Teacher
by Jay E. Adams   131pp. paperback

[handwritten: maintaining the delicate ... real once in christian living]

Here is a book that is long overdue. Carl Rogers convinced a generation of counselors to listen and reflect while insisting that teaching is taboo. Though Rogerianism failed, and is now largely passé, many counselors still hesitate to teach their counselees.

Dr. Adams shows not only that God obligates Christian counselors to teach, but how they may do so in ways that will help counselees both learn and "observe" those things that Christ "commanded" according to Matthew 28:20. He demonstrates clearly, using illustrations to which you will resonate, that effective biblical counseling requires teaching. This book, the only one of its kind, is must reading for every serious Christian.

Winning the War Within—
          A Biblical Strategy for Spiritual Warfare
by Jay E. Adams   151pp. paperback

Christian, you are at war! It is the battles at two levels—one outward, the other inward—that are our responsibilities as members of the church. While the outer battle is vital and pressing, it cannot be fought as it should be unless the Christian is successfully winning the war *within*. Do you know how to fight the war within? This book—reflecting the spirit of the Word of God—has been written to tell you in no uncertain terms that there is a way to victory. And, avoiding the path of mere theory, it explains how you, no matter how many times you have been defeated in the past, can begin to consistently win the battles within.

A Thirst For Wholeness
by Jay E. Adams   143pp. paperback

> How healthy is your spiritual integrity? Do your actions speak so loudly that people won't listen? *A Thirst for Wholeness* provides the solution to this common problem. Drawing on the book of James, Dr. Adams concentrates on how you can become a complete Christian from the inside out. As you study the inner dynamics involved in this process, you'll learn how to get your spiritual beliefs and your everyday actions in sync.

The Grand Demonstration—
A Biblical Study of the So-Called Problem of Evil
by Jay E. Adams   119pp. paperback

> Why is there sin, rape, disease, war, pain and death in a good God's world? Every Christian asks this question—but rarely receives an answer. Read this book and discover what God Himself says.

> *The Grand Demonstration* penetrates deeply into scriptural teaching regarding the nature of God. Moving into territory others fear to tread, Dr. Adams maintains that a fearless acceptance of biblical truth solves the so-called "problem of evil".

One Faithful Life

John MacArthur

Radio

One Perfect Life

The company is

Straight of

the Lord